Provoking
Poetry

Provoking Poetry

Natural Society

Jessica Hubbocks

Copyright © 2022 by Jessica Hubbocks

All rights reserved. No part of this book may be reproduced or used in any manner without written permission of the copyright owner except for the use of quotations in a book review.
For more information, email: provokingpoetrybook@outlook.com

FIRST EDITION

ILLUSTRATIONS & COVER BY ERIK MENDOZA

978-1-80227-500-1 (paperback)
978-1-80227-502-5 (hardcover)
978-1-80227-501-8 (ebook)

Prologue

Being able to gain access to wide variations of books and collections of poetry when I was younger inspired me to begin the writing process myself. I was influenced by multiple writers, like Wilfred Owen, John McCrae and Oscar Wilde, addressing issues within society through indirect and direct literature.

I wanted to create a small impact within society, just like these past authors did, through creative literature. My goal was to make it uncomplicated so that others can understand the hidden message behind every poem.

In the process of assembling my collection of poems, I discovered my own way of writing. Just being able to get lost within the thought process, truly being able to connect through pen and paper, demonstrating the true art of literature.

My vision was to be able to create and express my own thoughts whilst conveying strong and empowering messages to readers. These messages are intended to give others insights to a wiser self and let them envision a greater and smarter world with short impactful literature. I wanted to create a version of literature which would provoke a conversation; this way it would access people in a way a novel wouldn't.

I hope the poems start to make the reader question and understand the true reality within the world, stimulating their own thoughts, feelings and emotions. The world shows itself as being full of hatred, sleaze and destruction; however, there are glimpses of natural beauty behind everyone's mask.

The 4th

There is a guy who wholeheartedly holds a place within,
Never leaves and always tries to win,
Sometimes it's hard but he stays, even when I voice every sin
when never meaning a word,
Yet a defence for myself by trying to push you away,
Yet what I do sometimes gets too much.

I have always wanted you
here to stay,
Always and forever is what I say,
I have flaws and imperfections which cause dismay,
Yet I never want you to leave, okay?
I have tried for seven, nearly eight, months now,
But everything I do seems like it's never enough,
Not to win your heart,
Not for you to love me back,
I apologise for everything I have done,
While saying I miss you every single day,
I mean every action and word I say.

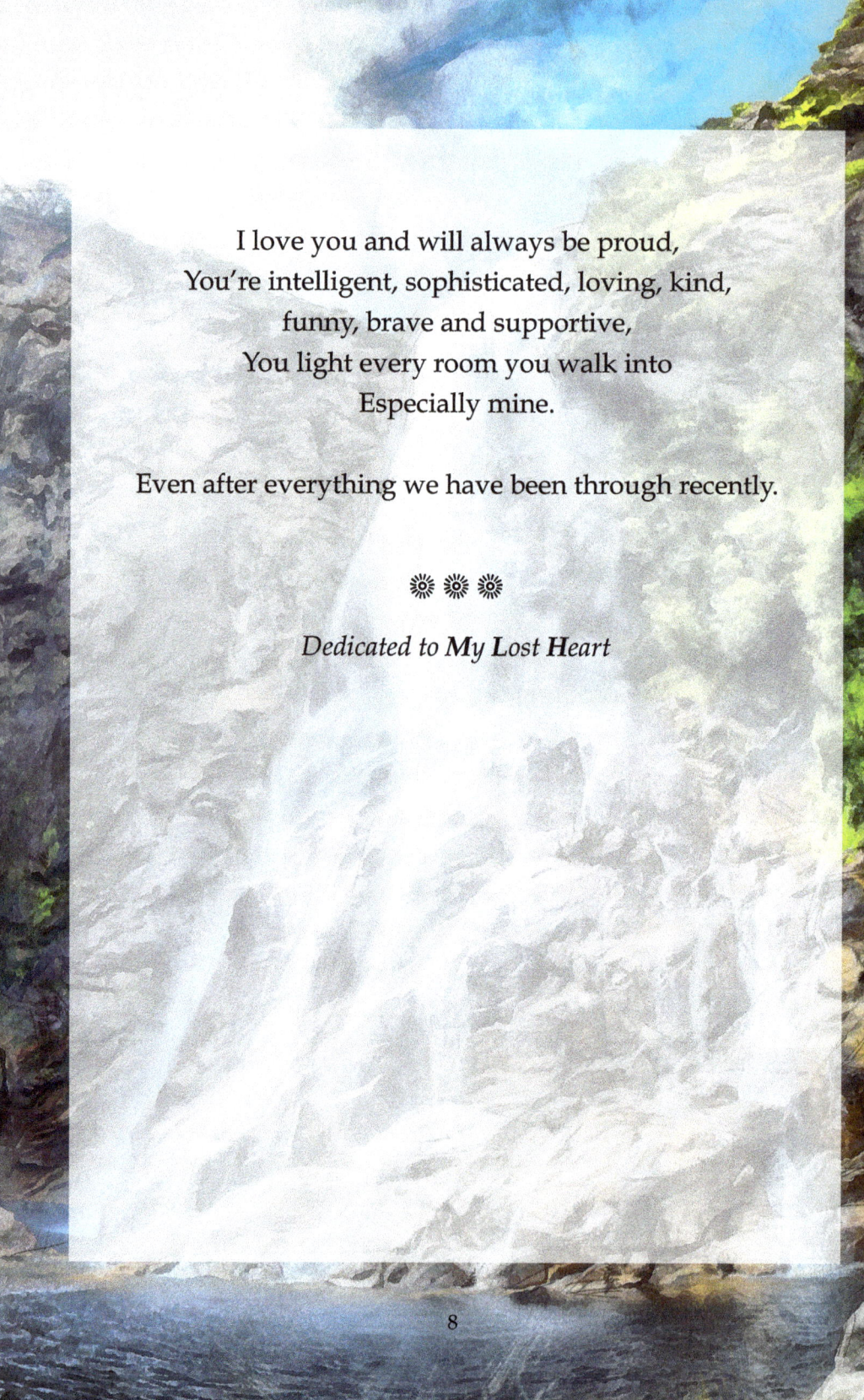

I love you and will always be proud,
You're intelligent, sophisticated, loving, kind,
funny, brave and supportive,
You light every room you walk into
Especially mine.

Even after everything we have been through recently.

❂ ❂ ❂

Dedicated to My Lost Heart

Beautiful Soul

A soul so bright like the sun,
Even in a winter breeze,
Like a kiss of the wind open for the November blow,
Focused within the positive,
Breathe within the glow.

Shining like a star at night
Within Orion's Belt,
Forcing the lines forming an unforgettable sign of a Libran.
A star to light up every December night,
Burning bright like magnesium's light.

Never forgotten, always merged into one's heart,
Never lost – always light,
Burn bright,
Burn bright,
On that cold, dark night,
Burn bright, burn bright.

Broke

Expansion.

The force between the long-winded breeze.

A black-and-white bird emerges from underneath the tree.

Resourceful yet wise. Brainy and sceptical.

The outed species searching for only glitter and gold.

The long-living aspiration of a significant culture.

Frantically rushing from tree to tree.

Human Life as we know it is substantially teaching

yet quick but a bird's life is longing yet vast

as their migration

Comprehension

Mentality is seen in many structures and builds,
Just like a neurological path,
Like finding a route conveniently mapped out,
Therefore shining a light towards that one trail
Specifically written for you.

Power,
Danger,
Creativity.

Damage

Being completely broken comes from nothing but external damage,
Started by family with constant vocal obligations,
Leading to friends breaking every piece of your already shattered trust.

Soon turning into nothing but outsiders,
Strangers just walking past,
Knowing nothing about your successes or opinions
Not knowing what your true character really is,
Not knowing who you really are,
Never being able to unmask anything but a facade worn to disguise your pain,
Forced into a constant internal scream,
Yet never spoken,
Growing and expanding internal pain.

Just damaged broken pieces of a soul,
Trying to mend itself,
Like shattered glass,
Unfixable; without a true kind soul wanting to support.

Searching for a way out of a place full of manipulative,
unknowing ignorance,
Climbing far out of a hole of destruction,
Leaving a place of complete disgrace,
Finding a place to finally call home.

Finally feeling nothing but happiness to be flying free
from nothing but evil,
Escaping like a bird's within a flock,
Feeling your complete personality.

Be brave enough to take the first step away from fakery and evil within this world. Put yourself first as your emotions matter within a society of bravery and courageousness.

Damn the Creation

Damn the creation beyond thy wandering eye,
Artistic values beaming across the sky,
Conquering to and fro,
Flooding thy countries,
Seen but always unknown,
From Marcus Aurelius,
A philosopher of life,
Braved by another
Caesar of light.

The Roman Empire, so powerful yet valiant,
Who conquered lands from Britain, Europe and the Middle East.

A strong and wise army
Using Greek philosophy,
Starting from pipe work to styles of architecture,
To rulers of animation,
Making an idea of power within a community.

Be the one to strike while the fire is hot, be brave and individual striving in your own uniqueness.

Days With You

I always think about you.
I think about looking forward to the future with you,
Finding both of us together,
Being happy,
Arguing but coming back together as soon as we realise
our wrongs.
It will be hard but we can grow to be perfect.

I was the one and only to you,
Your always and forever,
You were never going to let me go,
You wanted to keep me with you forever,
Yet you proved me right that you weren't going to stay.

Yet you love me still,
You want me still,
You say I am perfect still,
You say I'm pretty still.

Effort

Effort is needed in many areas,
Be it relationships,
People,
Work,
Friends.

Effort is required in many ways,
Through comfort,
Support,
Even trust and happiness.

It gets applied in everyday aspects.
So Support is important
as relying on yourself sometimes gets hard,
However, I have been doing things on my own for a while now,
Gotten used to it.

*Don't rely or need people,
Your own company is true beauty.*

Empty Promises

It all begins with words.
Words of affirmation that someone will do what they
promise,
All pinned down to
Belief, love and most importantly trust,
Trust hanging in the cruxes of your firm mind,
knowing that sometimes trust could be completely blind.

Facing Reality

Breathing in an air of nothing but fake auras,
Believing they are worthy propositions,
Embellished into nothing but a corrupted flower of lies,
Imbedded by a seed long ago planted
But never truly blossomed
Due to destruction of dead roots in the earth,
Only fighting to be free from this forsaken path.

Falling in Love

Falling in love doesn't last forever.

It can break but can make.

Love is never ending,

it's just a colossal.

Foundering

A physical failure to conceive,
Causing one to see it as punishment to oneself,
Only taking time to frantically breathe,
Consuming it all in,
No time to truly comprehend the severity of the situation,
Creating constant pressure to try to save or dispose half
of yourself,
Only praying that this depression wouldn't exist,
A simple action,
A big decision,
Out of your own hands,
A choice already made for you.

One life,
Gone
One hardship,
Created

One loss.

※ ※ ※

Help for women should be more available after miscarriages,
As it is seen to be demonised in our society,
Providing us no support.

Society should.

Let's help the women affected by this,
Both the mentally or physically vulnerable.

Friendship Drifts Over Time

Friendship drifts over time,
Turning into only fragments of grime,
Distancing from those once so special individuals,
Constantly loaning yourself to others as an inconsequential person,
Forming a friendship with only oneself.

Family and friendship as we know it become meaningless,
Heartache, pain and insignificant emotions hurt constantly,
Never being enough,
With the force of rhythm,
Time bears the low.

Egocentric, egotistical behaviour becomes inclined,
Transfixed as a bad quality.

Yet due to the hurt people caused,
They see you in a different light,
Wondering why you act and behave in a certain way.

※ ※ ※

Nevertheless, if they looked once at the actions they took maybe the questions needed would never have to be asked.

Greed

Mankind sourcing the life of redemption,
Over-consumption fuelling demise, sleaze and manipulation,
Defying the creation of selfish actions.
Almost like a reality in comparison.

Forces in need of complete contemplation.

Greed becomes the destruction of all evil,
Greed forcing the wild eyes upon power, land, money and food,
All to impress a community,
Not to invigorate self-pride,
But yet to consume outsourced validation,
Creating greed upon others and oneself,
Man making the outsource of greed.

A desire for something only man-made itself,
A greed for wealth and riches,
A greed to devour yet another repast,
A greed for complete control,
Wealth, food and power.
All outweighing the balance of morality, humility and kindness.

Greed is an unnecessary man-made issue,
So be kind to the ones around you,
Be less selfish and think about those less fortunate,
Believe in helping create a society of kindness which can fuel the wealth in our society
Leading us to disengage with class and status.
All will become meaningless.
Be the first to break that structure within society.

Love's Suffering

Heartbreak is as painful as demise,
The person you love has left,
Yet that one person is still alive,
Walking around,
Moving on and forgetting about you.

You become insignificant to their life,
Only distant memories,
Yet they fade over time,
So, memories become worthless.

Jogging someone's recollection of you,
Is relative to savouring a dementia mind.

Mass Media

Society moulded,
Consuming narratives that aren't sincere,
Written by one man,
Influencing public societal views and morals,
Formerly known as history.

The persistence of unknown sources,
Population starts to embellish the lies,
Absorbed constantly by the ignorant and naïve,
Words become constantly incoherent,
All just forming into deception.

Newspapers
Comics
Magazines
Pamphlets
All containing forgery.

*Read things carefully so you aren't manipulated
by the fakery that the media truly is.*

Natural Society

The wandered blissful eye,
Draws nakedly to peace,
The fragments starting so small,
The universe begins to grow.

Small places begin to form,
The change being so powerful,
Constant unknown pain continues, no matter how big or small,
Who?
Where?
Or how?
One soul binds to yours.

Love consumes all,
No matter what,
In just one look,
One smile,
One laugh
Or even one glance,
Everyone knows the bond is undeniable.

Love really does consume,
It draws you to the ecstasy and heroin of love,
The unknown drug that everyone sees, but never knows they need.

Don't fear the unexpected,
Take chances with the one,
One soul, one love, one laugh,
The one.

Be it me.

❃ ❃ ❃

*Dedicated to **My Lost Heart***

People

People are like lights,
Switching on and off,
Hopping from person to person
For their own gain.

Feelings start to become insignificant,
Love becomes entirely questioned,
And words become truly trivial.

Performance

People perform in different ways,
Showing their own beauty to others.
Talent shines,
Like a light shining strong onto another,
The sun,
A spotlight.
Finally created by a genius,
Thomas Edison, I say.

Power,
Beauty,
Framing.

They act in different ways,
You hope to be the stars,
Being swallowed is unfair,
Being damaged is unjust,
Being bold is powerful.

Pray

I pray thee passionate power,
I pray thee force drives,
I pray thee life lives,
Wanting this venting potential,
Fabricating the creation of a true individual.

We need to hold the ingenious solidity for people to
finally be great again.
Be it by heart,
Kindness,
Courage,
Passion,
Strength,
Or even through law.

Homelessness can be helped,
Deprivation can be solved,
Corruption forced out,
Education starting to strive,
Safety only a distant worry,
Poverty won't be established,
Wars will be fought.

Bold truths lie deeply within the society of the world.
But they will always be forgotten by higher powers.

Things should solve themselves by the true independent, strong-minded souls.

Rumours

All started by an insignificant individual,
Imbedding the epitome of stupidity,
All fuelled from nothing but lies,
Causing the rumours to corrupt society,
Scaring another like a burn from lava,
Breaking another into complete destruction,
Too cowardly to brave someone's face,
Answer, reply, confrontation,
Leaving only them on higher ground.

Everything leans which seems to be preposterous,
Making others consume lies,
Scaring your identity,
Learn to realise others will constantly try to put you down,
Making you seem corrupt, showing their real mask,
Become brave, strong and inattentive,
Making them weak.

*Forget the resignation and empower oneself for the better.
Be empowered by people who would try to destroy what you
are due to misconception, jealousy and insecurity complexes.
Be brave, confident and wise.*

She wouldn't dare go thorugh with it

that she did?

You'll ne...

did you see her?

did you see her?

is a total liar

Speak Up

Speak up,
Speak loud,
Speak proud,
Stand out from the entire crowd,
Empower oneself with the sound of one's voice,
Bravery and striking strength banishing the immoral,
Bringing in full determination.

Which inspires others,
Be that guiding light,
Enflame that burning desire inside,
Enhance the creation of suspected perfection,
Find the receipts of no one.

Your own opinion
Wraps the judgement for others,
Gratification, satisfaction, contentment,
Filling the shoes of power,
Opinion and less corruption.

Speak up when things are wrong. Speak loud to vocalise deception. Speak proud defining the confidence within.

Strength

Strength isn't power,
It starts to slowly change into weakness,
Flaws are the true power,
Consumed by your own mind.

Potential is sought within,
Within the fragments of your own sources,
Amend the fire within,
Agreed with stubbornness.

The 24th

A man born on a day of pure grace,
Bringing nothing but light laughter,
Filling a room with complete safety,
Complete purity seen within a soul which is a rarity,
Showing the true wonders within society,
Living. Loving. Laughing.
A man of complete honour and humility,
Brightening every soul within a dark room,
A true lightness shining like a star at night,
Forming a guidance for a worthy individual.

A man soulfully missed,
A man of true greatness,
A man who stood out breaking the mask within society,
Nothing but pure kindness,
A man so longed for in today's world,
Yet completely irreplaceable.

A poem for my grandpapa

The Capsules

One... maybe two... three,
Four... five... six...
Seven isn't enough,
Let's go to eight,
A glass,
Eight tablets,
Thinking the end is near.

Thinking the end is only a footstep away,
Once never,
Just twice.
It should be solved by support even the first time,
No resolution for two.

Suicidal thoughts continuously passing like mad cars at rush hour.

The severity of mental health should be supported at the first sight of change in someone's behaviour.

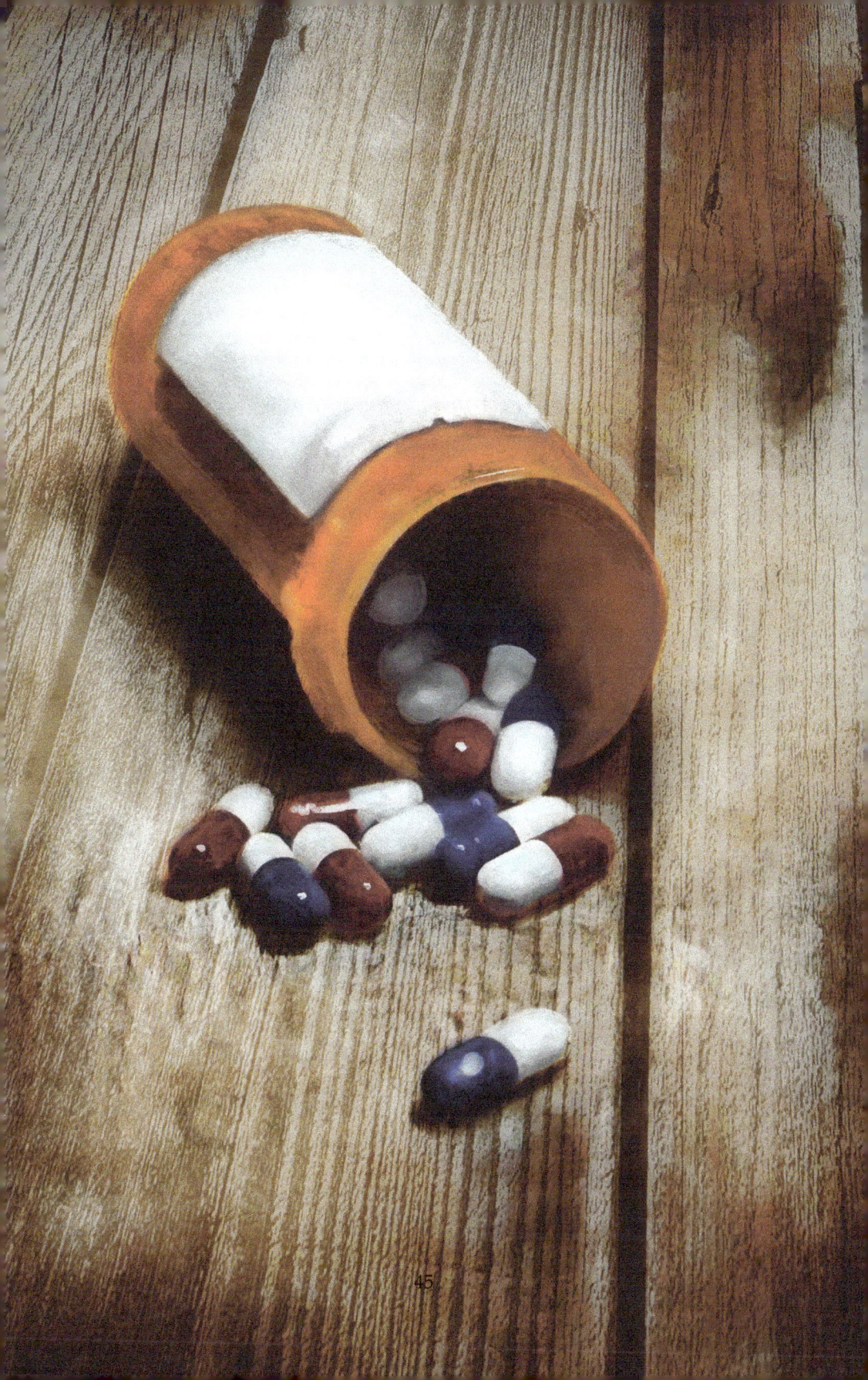

The Idea of Love

Love is something that takes over you,
Makes you feel a certain way,
Something you have never felt before,
So, you hold onto that feeling,
Holding onto that person who makes you feel that special way.

In the end, you will eventually get hurt.
It's only when they don't want you,
You get hurt and feel so alone,
Nothing else will feel the same as before,
Love is painful but consuming.

Why is love so drastic but amazing at the same time?

You still feel intensely for that one person,
They consumed you like no other,
Let them go because fighting for someone to love you and want you is never the answer.

Why fight if they felt the way they said before?
You'd think they would be willing to commit and
understand your feelings and love you no matter what
the circumstance.

Let them love you, not the other way around.

If they have fallen out of love,
Pain will start to kick in,
Just stop trying for something that will never change
their mind.

They will realise what they lost themselves in time.

The Ruiner

A person so damned from the outsourced evil,
A monstrosity of humankind,
Truly corrupting another with just one word,
One thought,
Completely broken in entirety due to outsourced manipulation.

Thoughts

Constant thoughts processing everything at once,
Process after process,
A state of emergency drawing over you,
Suicidal thoughts fly over like a plane, searching for a criminal,
You,
Your thoughts,
One knife.

Wanting to take your own life,
Wanting the pain to stop,
Wanting people to notice you change,
Wanting at least one recognition.

Never seen.

Just wants and needs that bruise you
Over time,
Finally searching,
Looking for clarity,

To help every thought that's just pacing,
Wandering like a star,
Fiercely shining bright every night.

Breathe,
Replace,
Think.

Think about the good times and not the problems you are trying to solve at this moment in time.

Unrequited Love

Preordained over one individual,
Loving and passionately admiring,
Consumed by notability,
Suspicions of them feeling the same,
Yet it's just sentiment from one side,
One side truly appreciating the other,
Boldly believing there will be no one better,
So, you wait,
Seeing what the future contains for your love life.

Hoping,
Merely wishing for something substantial,
Belief,
Faith and desire.

If it is meant to be with the one person you wish it with, it will be true love. Just keep believing in yourself and things will come to you.

Waiting

Waiting… waiting… waiting…
Impatient people begin to fall like dominos,
Piling down in constant thuds,
Time trying to source itself,
Turning into fractions of people.

Impatient minds hold power,
To control their true weaknesses,
This being resignation,
The clock holds the bearer of bad news,
from their constant complaining.

www.ingramcontent.com/pod-product-compliance
Lightning Source LLC
Chambersburg PA
CBHW041153110526
44590CB00027B/4213